D0913224

What Are Castles and Knights?

by Sarah Fabiny

illustrated by Dede Putra

Penguin Workshop

For everyone who has come
to my aid in battle—SF

PENGUIN WORKSHOP
An imprint of Penguin Random House LLC, New York

First published in the United States of America by Penguin Workshop,
an imprint of Penguin Random House LLC, New York, 2022

Visit us online at penguinrandomhouse.com.

Library of Congress Control Number: 2021049014

Printed in the United States of America

ISBN 9780593226865 (paperback)   10 9 8 7 6 5 4 3 2 1 WOR
ISBN 9780593226872 (library binding)   10 9 8 7 6 5 4 3 2 1 WOR

Contents

What Are Castles and Knights?

Stirling Castle in Scotland was built on high rocks and had thick walls. It was supposed to withstand an attack from any enemy army. But King Edward I of England had other ideas, and he was not going to let high rocks and thick walls stop him from taking the castle. Edward and his

army had been fighting the Scots for years in the Scottish Wars of Independence. Stirling Castle was one of the few castles left in Scottish control, and Edward was determined to seize it.

In April 1304, Edward had a message delivered to the castle. The message said that an army of more than 1,500 soldiers and knights was on its way to attack. The castle was under the control of Sir William Oliphant, and he had only about

twenty-five men there with him. However, they had expected an attack and were prepared. They had stocked the caves under the castle with salted meat and fish, dried fruit, and sacks of flour and grain. There was also a well beneath the castle that would provide fresh water. Up on the high walls of the castle, the defenders got ready for the siege. They armed themselves with bows and arrows and crossbows.

The English army brought thirteen trebuchets (a type of catapult that uses gravity and a counterweight). They hoped these weapons would smash the thick walls of Stirling Castle. The army fired rocks and fireballs at the castle day and night. Against all odds, Stirling Castle held out through the siege. However, after four months, the defenders' supplies were running low, and they were exhausted by the nonstop attacks. But William Oliphant and his men were not willing to admit defeat.

The English army firing a trebuchet

Little did William Oliphant and his men know that the worst was yet to come! The English army had built the biggest trebuchet the world had ever seen. It was called the Warwolf. This giant weapon, which could fling a rock weighing three hundred pounds, soon destroyed one of the castle walls. Sir William knew that the castle was no match for this fearsome weapon, and he and his men would have to surrender.

King Edward I agreed to let Sir William and his men surrender, but he also wanted to humiliate them. He ordered all the defenders to march out of the castle barefoot and with ashes on their faces. They were sent to England as prisoners, and Sir William Oliphant was locked up in the Tower of London.

We usually think of castles as places where life was carefree, with kings and queens and royalty feasting and knights in armor practicing sword fighting. While those things did happen, life in the High Middle Ages was pretty hard. People feared attacks from neighboring kingdoms, and they wanted to be safe. The strong, sturdy structure of a castle protected them from enemies, and brave, skilled knights went to battle to guarantee this protection.

Sir William Oliphant locked up in the Tower of London

CHAPTER 1
Loyalty and Protection

In the period we call the Middle Ages—a period from about AD 500 to 1500—there were no nations in Europe. Countries such as France, Spain, Germany, and Italy didn't exist yet. Instead, powerful lords ruled over this territory. These lords each had their own land (their domain), and at the center of each domain was a castle. Lords were often at war with one another. They

Britain composed of dukedoms and smaller domains

attacked rivals, hoping to take over the land, the castle, and everything in it.

To fight against enemies, every lord supported a group of knights. Knights were soldiers who went to battle on horseback. No one without a horse could become a knight.

Although they weren't paid, the knights got to live at the lord's castle for free. Food and clothing were free, too. Horses were very expensive; sometimes a lord had to buy a horse for a poorer knight. Knights fought in protective gear called armor. A suit of armor cost a lot to make. Often the lord had to pay for knights' armor as well. Knights, along with foot soldiers and archers (people who fight with bows and arrows), helped defend the lord's castle against attacks. Or, if the lord wanted, they went on attack, hoping to seize another lord's castle and land.

Who farmed all the lord's land?

That job fell to peasants called serfs, who lived outside the castle on the lord's estate. Peasants also

looked after the lord's herds of animals. Peasants received no pay, but they were given a place to live and could keep part of the crops to feed their families.

In return for everybody's service—soldiers as well as peasants—the lord provided protection. This system was known as feudalism. In Western Europe, feudalism lasted for hundreds of years. It reached its height between the 1000s and 1300s, a period often called the High Middle Ages.

As time went on, neighboring lords banded together for mutual protection. The richest and most powerful lord in the group—usually the one with the most knights—became king. The other lords pledged loyalty to the king, and he provided them with safety and security. However, fighting still continued among these larger groups.

Eventually the various kings banded together or were conquered by their enemies until a very large area had just one king. This was the beginning of countries, as well as large-scale wars among countries.

Where Does the Word *Knight* Come From?

The word *knight* comes from the Anglo-Saxon word *cniht*. *Cniht* means servant or attendant. It is a reminder that it was a knight's duty to serve his lord. He had to be ready to go to battle whenever his king or lord called on him. The English used the word to describe the French soldiers who came to England when William the Conqueror invaded in 1066. These French soldiers rode on horseback. In many languages, the word for knight describes a soldier on horseback: in French, *chevalier*; in German, *ritter*; in Italian, *cavaliere*; and in Spanish, *caballero*.

CHAPTER 2
My Home, My Castle

The greatest symbol of life during the High Middle Ages was the castle. The word *castle* comes from the Latin word *castellum*, which means small fort. That's exactly what a castle was.

We usually think of castles as the homes of kings and queens and nobility where feasts, festivals, jousting matches, and archery competitions took place. While castles were places where royalty lived and enjoyed ceremonies and feasts, that wasn't their main purpose. During the High Middle Ages, there was so much local warfare that, more than anything, a castle's key function was to protect the people who lived inside and outside it.

Castles were usually constructed on high ground and next to a river or lake. Due to their location on high ground, a castle was difficult to attack. Being near a river or lake provided not only a water supply but also a transportation route. A castle was a symbol of power and showed the might of the lord who owned it. Castles were meant to scare off enemies, but castles were also homes and served as the seat of government for a lord's estate.

The earliest castles built in Europe were a type called motte and bailey (say: maht and BAY-lee). They were made of wood and earth. The builders made a large, steep mound of dirt (the motte). Below the motte was a large area that was surrounded by a high fence and a ditch (the bailey).

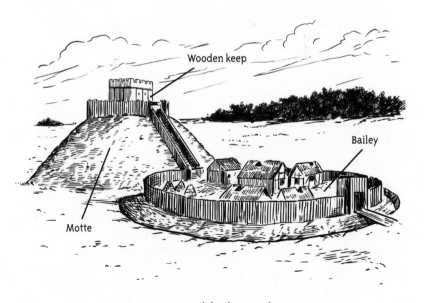

Motte-and-bailey castle

At the top of the motte was a wooden tower, or keep. Around a hundred people might live in a motte-and-bailey castle, and the keep was where they would take shelter if under attack. The keep was usually surrounded by a tall wall or fence. Because the keep was at the top of a steep hill, it was difficult to attack. It was also easy to defend, as an approaching enemy could be seen from far away.

Workshops and stables were located in the bailey. The barracks where the lord's knights lived were also in the bailey. There might also be a church, a kitchen, and a great hall used for celebrations and feasts.

Around 1100, castles began to be built out of stone and keeps became round in shape. Stone castles were much sturdier and stronger than wood and earth castles. Round keeps made it easier for people defending the castle to see in all directions. And round keeps could deflect rocks and arrows better than square keeps. Though stone castles were expensive to build, they offered better protection and could not be burned down. Over the next few hundred years, stone castles became more grand and more elaborate.

Construction of Alnwick Castle in England began around 1100.

Stone castles usually had two or more rings of walls around them. This made it very hard for attackers to invade. The inner walls were higher so that defenders could see their attackers. It also allowed them to fire weapons and shoot arrows over the heads of other defenders on the outer wall.

A "Modern" Castle

Pembroke Castle is located in western Wales. It was built on a rocky point that juts into the Pembroke River. Surrounded by water on three sides, the castle began as a simple motte-and-bailey structure in the late eleventh century. But over the next one hundred years, it suffered

several attacks and sieges, and the castle was rebuilt. It is one of the best examples of a stone castle from the High Middle Ages.

Pembroke Castle has a massive round keep that is nearly eighty feet high, with walls that are almost twenty feet thick at the base. The keep also has a domed roof that once supported a fighting platform. The platform was built to allow the castle's defenders to go out past the keep's walls and be above the heads of attackers.

The castle has a gatehouse with large towers and several portcullises that did an excellent job of keeping attackers out. The castle is also built over a cavern that was protected by a wall and a barred gateway. The cave served as a port for ships and as a storeroom.

Henry VII, the father of Henry VIII and the grandfather of Elizabeth I, was born at Pembroke Castle.

Sometimes a large ditch called a moat surrounded the outer wall of the castle. A moat might be filled with water or tall spikes. A drawbridge could be raised and lowered over the moat, and it was raised whenever the castle was attacked. Behind the drawbridge was a spiked wooden or metal barrier called a portcullis.

A portcullis

It protected the thick, heavy doors behind it from battering rams and fire. The portcullis was raised and lowered by chains or ropes from a room above the gateway. All these were not meant to keep people in; they were to keep people out.

Even though castles were built as fortresses, they were also homes. These homes may have looked grand, but they often weren't very comfortable and there wasn't much privacy. In the winter, castles were very cold and drafty, especially in the northern part of Europe, and it was difficult to keep them warm. An open fire in the middle or corner of a room was the source of heat. (Fireplaces weren't invented until the eleventh or twelfth century.) There wasn't anything like insulation in those days, so tapestries (large woven hangings) were hung on the walls. They kept the castle warm, and they also gave color and beauty to the drab stone walls. Tapestries could also be rolled up and easily moved from room to room or castle to castle.

The Unicorn Tapestries

The Unicorn Tapestries comprise a series of large tapestries that together tell the story of a hunt for a magical unicorn. Each of the complete tapestries measures twelve feet tall and up to fourteen feet wide. They are some of the most beautiful and detailed tapestries ever made. They make you feel as if you could walk right into them.

The Unicorn Tapestries were made between 1495 and 1505. Who first owned them?

That's a mystery. The initial *A* entwined with a backward *E* appears several times on the tapestries. Perhaps they were a wedding gift to a couple whose first names began with those letters. Today, the Unicorn Tapestries hang in the Cloisters, a museum in New York City.

The great hall was the area where daily business of the lord took place. It was also where everyone ate and slept except for the lord and his wife. Their living quarters were usually on the top floor of the keep. Castles had a large kitchen, usually in a separate building or the basement, as well as a chapel, storerooms, workshops, stables, and a well. Toilets were a bit like an indoor outhouse. They consisted of a seat called a garderobe (say: GARD-robe) built into the thick walls of the castle. The seat was over a chute that led to pits below—or into the moat. And there was no toilet paper. People used hay instead. The floors in a castle were bare wood or stone, and they were covered with sweet-

A medieval castle toilet

smelling hay instead of carpets or rugs. The hay helped cover up the stinky smell of a castle.

Even though castles could be dark and damp and dirty, that didn't stop the people living there from having celebrations. The celebrations were often feasts that marked important events or holidays.

At a feast, the lord sat at the high table. The table was on a raised platform so that the lord could see everyone and they could see him. Any important guests visiting the lord would also sit at the high table. Everyone else sat at long tables. The food served at a feast was usually different kinds of meat or game, fish, cheese, fruit, and pastries. On a very special occasion, a roasted swan or even a peacock might be served. People ate with their hands and shared plates and bowls of food. They often ate off slabs of stale bread called trenchers. While eating, guests were entertained

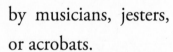

by musicians, jesters, or acrobats.

Feasts were a good way for a lord to keep everyone in the castle happy. They also kept knights out of fights with one another!

CHAPTER 3
So You Want to Be a Knight

Not anyone could become a knight. There were very strict rules about who was allowed to train as one. By the twelfth century, it was unusual for anyone who wasn't the son of a knight to become one himself. Even if someone went through the training, it still didn't automatically mean he became a knight.

A knight-in-training had to prove that he was fit for the job. He had to show that he could use a range of weapons and handle a horse. They had to be fearless fighters, honorable, and loyal subjects to their lord. But that wasn't all. Knights were supposed to be generous to the poor as well as kind to all, especially women.

In a lord's family, the oldest son usually stayed home because one day he would take over his father's castle, title, and property.

Younger sons of a lord became knights. When a boy turned seven, he'd usually be sent to live at the castle of another noble—usually an uncle or a friend of his father. There he'd begin his training.

Not Just a Boys' Club

While women were not allowed to have the title of knight, there were a few women who performed the duties of a knight and fought in battles. These are some of them:

Matilda of Canossa (1046–1115): She was a countess in Tuscany (Italy) and often fought in armor, leading her troops in battles between the Pope and the Holy Roman Emperor.

Joanna of Flanders (c. 1295–1374): When Hennebont, in northern France, was under attack, she led three hundred men out of the town. They attacked the enemy camp and burned it down.

And the most famous is:

Joan of Arc (c. 1412–1431): In 1429, she convinced the French ruler, Charles VII, to give her an army to help the city of Orléans, which was under attack. She was able to free the city in just a few days.

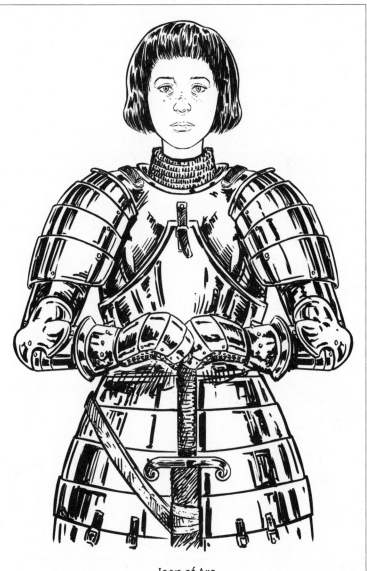

Joan of Arc

A knight-in-training started as a page. He had basic lessons in writing and reading, was taught manners and how to be polite, and he also learned how to serve food at mealtime.

A lot of a page's training was just spent watching how life in the castle worked and how other knights behaved. He also spent some time learning archery, horsemanship, and weapons skills. Was the training all about fighting? No. Pages also learned how to hunt and to play chess, ball games, and music.

When a knight-in-training turned fourteen, he became a squire and was an apprentice to one knight in particular. (An apprentice is a young boy who works for somebody else to learn a skill or trade.) As a squire, he was expected to serve his knight—he cared for the knight's horse and armor, he waited on the knight at the table during meals, and he even followed the knight into battles.

When a squire was not waiting on his knight, he had to go through more intense battle training. Not every squire was able to complete it. He had to learn how to run while wearing heavy armor, practice hitting a quintain (a target that spun around) with a heavy lance while riding a horse, and have mock fights with other squires using wooden swords and shields.

A squire practices hitting a quintain

After about five years, if a squire successfully completed this training, he was allowed to become a knight. (Sometimes squires were made knights on a battlefield if they had showed great bravery.) The ceremony for knighthood was called a dubbing.

The ceremony started with the squire taking a bath to clean his body and purify his soul. He then sat up through the night, praying in the castle chapel.

In the morning, he had breakfast with his family and friends. Afterward, two knights dressed him in a white tunic (a long, loose fitting shirt) with a white belt. White was chosen because it stood for purity.

He also wore black or brown stockings, which represented the earth to which he would one day return. Finally, a scarlet cloak, red for the blood that he was prepared to shed in battle, was wrapped around him. Then the knight-to-be knelt in front of his lord and was tapped on the neck or shoulders with a hand or a sword. This tap was meant to be the only "blow" the knight would ever receive without fighting back. Once the new knight had taken his vows, he was presented with his own sword and spurs as symbols of his new role. The dubbing was often followed by a feast and dancing.

Modern-Day Knights

Several countries, including England, Italy, France, and Spain, still award men with the title of knight. They are given this title not because they are brave soldiers, but because of service to their country in the arts, entertainment, government, or military. Elton John, Paul McCartney, Mick Jagger, and Bono have all been knighted by Queen Elizabeth II, which means they can use the title Sir.

Sir Elton John

Women can be awarded the same type of honor, and then can use the title Dame. Olivia Newton-John, Maggie Smith, Twiggy, and Emma Thompson are all dames.

CHAPTER 4
Get Your Armor On

A knight needed more than a sword, stirrups, and a horse to perform his duties, especially if he had to go into battle. He needed armor that would protect him from arrows, swords, lances, spears, clubs, axes, and all the other weapons that were used on the medieval battlefield.

Arrow   Sword   Lance

Before the 1300s, chain mail armor was common. Over a padded tunic called a pourpoint or aketon, a knight wore a coat called a hauberk (say: HAW-berk) made of hundreds of small iron rings linked together. Pieces of chain mail armor were also made to go over a knight's legs and arms. Chain mail was heavy; the weight of it hung from a knight's shoulders. But it was flexible and provided fairly good protection. The problem was that chain mail could be pierced by an arrow or the thin blade of a sword,

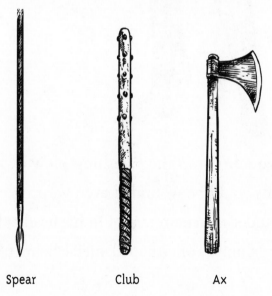

Spear   Club   Ax

and wouldn't stop the smashing blow of a club.
Knights could be wounded even wearing padded
vests under the chain mail. On his head, a knight
wore a simple cone-shaped metal helmet with a

metal strip that came down over his nose (later helmets covered the whole head). He carried a shield for protection and a long spear called a lance. The shield was usually made of wood covered with heavy leather and strips of iron.

Each knight also wore a tunic over his armor. On the tunic was a design (crest) that stood for his family. The same crest appeared on the shield that the knight carried into battle. The crest and the colors that a knight and his family used were called a coat of arms. A coat of arms was passed down from a father to his oldest son. Other sons in the family used different versions of their father's coat of arms.

A coat of arms

A coat of arms served a practical purpose, too. Because helmets covered a knight's head, crests and coats-of-arms were a way to tell friend from foe on the battlefield.

At first, blacksmiths made armor for knights. But as time went on, knights wanted more protective armor, and they needed skilled craftsmen to create it. By the 1300s, workshops of these skilled craftsmen, called armorers, were using new techniques to make armor lighter and also withstand most weapons on a battlefield. Chain mail was replaced by full suits of armor made from twenty or more separate pieces. The plates covered a knight's entire body, from the

An armorer

sabatons on his feet and the breastplate on his chest, to the gauntlets on his hands and the bevor on his neck.

A suit of armor had joints so that the knight could move easily in battle and use his weapons. It could weigh more than fifty pounds, and a knight needed help from a squire to put it on.

The Knights of Japan

Like nobles and lords in Europe, nobles and lords in Japan had knights to help protect their lands. In Japan, these knights were called samurai.

The samurai became more and more powerful, and in 1185, one of the samurai gained control of all Japan. He took the title of shogun. Even though Japan had an emperor, the real power lay with the shogun and the samurai.

The samurai followed a set of rules called Bushido (say: BU-shih-doh), which means "way of the warrior." The rules stated that a samurai must be brave and honest, must be a skillful soldier, and must honor his parents. Above all, a samurai must obey his leader.

A samurai's armor was made from small pieces of leather, steel, and wood that were laced together with silk or fabric. These pieces were then coated with lacquer. The lacquer served as a protective coating that also gave the armor a shiny appearance.

The pieces of armor went on in a special order, and once the full suit was on properly, a knight was able to run, fight, and ride his horse. However, it was very hot in a suit of armor. And hard to hear anything when a helmet was worn.

Was a suit of armor expensive?

Yes! Very!

There were also pieces of armor made for horses. They usually covered its face, neck, chest, and hindquarters. A horse that was ridden into battle was called a destrier or "strong horse." Battles were loud and confusing, and a knight and his horse were partners on the battlefield.

With a word or a gesture, a well-trained horse would turn or circle, rear up and strike attackers, or bite enemy horses.

If he was wealthy enough, a knight might own more than one horse. He might have separate horses for hunting and jousting (a courser), traveling (a rouncey), and carrying baggage (a sumpter).

Sumpter horse

Being a knight and riding into battle was an honor, but it was an expensive one.

CHAPTER 5
Into Battle

Every knight hoped that one day he would charge into battle wearing his armor. It was what he had spent nearly his whole life training for.

On the battlefield, a knight's goal was to knock an enemy off his horse, leaving him unprotected. But he also needed to protect himself from enemy blows. To do this, a knight on horseback needed a weapon that he could swing and move quickly. Besides a sword, a knight might carry a small lance, a battle-ax, or a mace. (A mace is a short wooden stick with a heavy metal head at one end.) These weapons could pierce through the joints in an enemy's armor or deliver bone-crushing blows. And of course, a knight always carried his shield, which displayed his coat of arms.

A knight in armor on a horse was like an armored tank. He was able to move quickly, knock enemies off their horses, and smash through lines of foot soldiers. But if a knight in armor fell from his horse, he was in trouble. It was hard for him to get back on his horse. And if his horse was injured, killed, or ran off, he was then an easy target for the enemy.

Stirrups and Saddles

There were two things that helped knights on horseback: stirrups and a saddle. With his feet in stirrups, a knight could control his horse better. Using pressure from his legs, he was able to let his horse know quickly whether to move forward or back, right or left. Plus, a knight had more power when he stood up in his stirrups. He could swing his weapon more easily and effectively.

A knight's saddle had a high front (a pommel) and a high back (a cantle). This helped keep a knight on his horse if a weapon hit him or if he had landed a hard blow on an enemy.

Very often, a knight who had been unhorsed wouldn't be killed. He could be worth more alive than dead. A fallen knight might be taken prisoner and held at the enemy lord's castle. The enemy lord would then ask the knight's lord to pay a ransom for his release. (A ransom is something paid or demanded for the freedom of a captured person.) Sometimes it was years before the ransom money could be paid.

Knights on horseback were often accompanied by foot soldiers. These foot soldiers were either squires training as knights, knights who couldn't afford a horse, or peasants who were forced to fight by their lord. They usually carried long spears called pikes, halberds (long spears with an ax at the end), or bows and arrows.

A group of foot soldiers would stand close together with their weapons facing forward. Very often they could hold off an enemy charge of horses. No knight wanted his horse to be injured or killed by running into a line of pikes or being shot by arrows.

A lord commanding a battle hoped the initial charge would defeat his enemy and make them retreat. Knights in a charge had to work as a team—not only the men, but the horses as well.

If the initial charge wasn't successful, the knights had to regroup and prepare for a second charge. By that time, the enemy may have sent out a charge. Or foot soldiers may have advanced. A lord who was able to keep his knights, their horses, and his foot soldiers disciplined during the chaos often won a battle.

It didn't only matter how many knights and foot soldiers a lord took into battle and what kinds of weapons they used. The location of the battle was also important. A skilled leader would try to get the better position before a battle.

Weapons of War

Knights might have some of the following: a mace, a war hammer, a battle-ax, a morning star, a military flail, and a great sword.

Mace   War hammer   Morning star   Military flail

Armed foot soldiers used a halberd, a gisarme or a glaive, and a longbow or a crossbow.

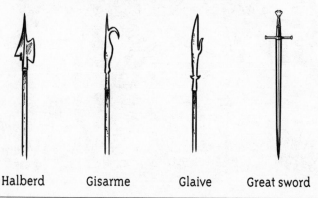

Halberd   Gisarme   Glaive   Great sword

He would want to be on higher ground so that he could see the enemy more easily. This also meant his army would run downhill rather than uphill. Or a commanding lord might position his army so that the enemy had to charge through mud or water. All of that slowed down an enemy and made it more difficult for them to move quickly into a battle.

The Battle of Agincourt

The Hundred Years' War was a long conflict, fought between England and France from 1337 to 1453. The two countries fought over who had the right to rule France. One of the most famous battles of that war is the Battle of Agincourt, fought on October 25, 1415.

Even though the English army was outnumbered, they won the battle. King Henry V of England sailed to France with about twelve thousand soldiers, but by the time he reached Agincourt, he was down to about six thousand.

King Henry V

66

The French army that met them had four times as many soldiers. Henry positioned his men at the edge of a field that had recently been plowed. The French had to cross this muddy field, and during the charge, the French army's horses got stuck in the mud. Many of the French knights had to dismount. Since they were in heavy armor, it was also hard for them to get through the mud. The English had brought many archers with them to the battle, and the French were easy targets for their arrows. More than five thousand French soldiers were killed, including many princes and nobles, but the English lost only 113 men.

CHAPTER 6
Attack!

Besides meeting their enemies on the battlefield, knights also attacked the castles of enemy lords. While a castle was built to be a fortress that kept friends in and foes out, there were ways to make it fall or get its occupants to surrender. Taking another lord's castle and everything in it was a sign of power and might. It was the grand prize in the Middle Ages.

A catapult

An attack on a castle was a big operation. A lord needed a large army of knights and lots of different kinds of weapons. The knights didn't need their horses for a siege on a castle, but they did need to know how to use these weapons. They very often also needed patience.

An attacking army would set up camp outside the castle it planned to attack. It might take them days or weeks—or even months—to vanquish a castle. So a camp served as the headquarters for the attack.

One of the first things an attacking army did was cut off supplies to the castle. They either burned the surrounding farmland or prevented the lord's serfs from delivering food, fuel, and water. Without these essential supplies, it was hard for those inside the castle to last very long. Castles usually kept large stores of food and water in case of sieges, but often the attack lasted longer than the supplies. Once a camp was set up and supplies were cut off, the army would attack the castle itself.

A moat made it difficult for soldiers to get their large weapons close to the castle walls. But an attacking army had ways of dealing with moats. If a moat was filled with water, an attacking army might cross it by using small boats or build a footpath by dumping wood, stones, and rocks into part of it. If a moat contained sharp spikes, it was difficult to get through,

but an attacking army could cut them down.

Sometimes it was easier to go under the castle walls than over them. So an attacking army often tried to dig under the walls. They weren't really trying to crawl under the thick walls. They were hoping that digging a hole under the wall would make the wall collapse. If the wall did collapse, an attacking army could charge inside.

Knights using a battering ram

As some attacking soldiers were digging, others used battering rams to break down the gates and ladders and siege towers to get over the walls. A siege tower was a tall wooden structure on wheels that could be rolled up to the castle walls. The walls of the tower protected the attackers inside as they made their way to the castle.

Other soldiers fired heavy stones from catapults and trebuchets (say: TREH-byoo-shet), which were like huge slingshots. These weapons needed several men to fire them. The stones they shot at the castle could weigh up to three hundred pounds.

Trebuchet

One of the most destructive weapons an attacking army used was called a bombard. It was a large cannon that fired big stone or metal balls. The balls did a lot of damage to the walls of a castle, as well as to everything inside the walls. Bombards were one of the first weapons to use gunpowder to fire their missiles. They were heavy and hard to move, so eventually they were replaced by cannons that were smaller and lighter.

But soldiers in the castle weren't sitting ducks. They had ways and weapons to defend themselves. Because they were on higher ground, defending soldiers had a good view of their attackers. They used this position to their advantage. From up above, soldiers on the castle walls were well placed to fire arrows out of narrow slits in the walls and dump barrels of hot water on soldiers below. They also used smaller catapults that could be moved around the tops of the castle walls.

Stirling Castle in Scotland

A motte-and-bailey castle layout

A medieval toilet

Statue of Joan of Arc

Queen Elizabeth II knights Captain Sir Thomas Moore.

Armor on display at the Philadelphia Museum of Art

A coat of arms

The dungeon of Greillenstein Castle in Austria

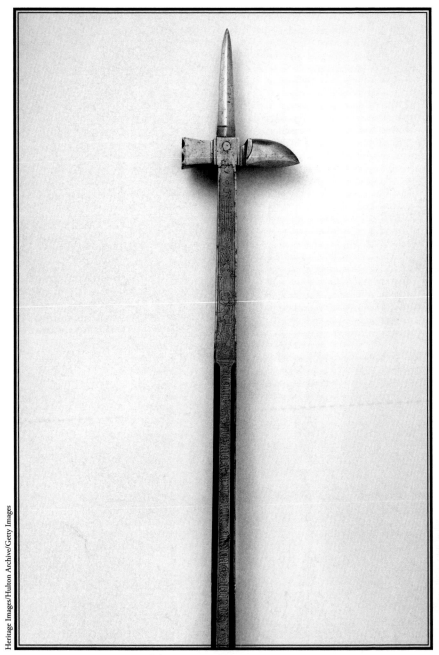

A fifteenth-century war hammer

A trebuchet

The Mons Meg cannon at Edinburgh Castle in Scotland

Kenilworth Castle in England

Two knights joust with lances.

Eilean Donan Castle in Scotland

These smaller catapults, called mangonels and
onagers (say: MANG-guh-nel and ON-uh-jer),
often shot flaming missiles at the attacking army.
Soldiers hoped the flames would set the siege
towers on fire.

The Siege of Kenilworth Castle

The longest siege on a castle in England was at Kenilworth Castle. It started on June 25, 1266 and ended on December 13, 1266—that's 172 days, almost six months. It began when King Henry III attacked rebels led by Henry de Hastings. The king had given Simon de Montfort's family the castle, but when Simon's family decided to oppose the king, the king decided he wanted the castle back. Simon had been killed in battle, but Henry de Hastings and his men continued the fight.

The castle was surrounded by a wide moat, so the king's army wasn't able to get their siege towers close to the castle. The catapults weren't powerful enough to throw stones over the moat and hit the castle walls with enough force to break through. The king brought barges to take his army across the moat, but the defenders in the castle sank them.

The king's weapons weren't able to do any damage, but after such a long time of being trapped in the castle, it was hunger and sickness that ended the siege. With only days' worth of food left, the defenders surrendered—and the king got his castle back.

Kenilworth Castle

Mons Meg

One of the largest bombards ever built and used is the Mons Meg. It was built in 1449 and given as a gift to King James II of Scotland in 1454. It was used in castle sieges until the middle of the sixteenth century. Mons Meg weighed 15,366 pounds (that's more than an African elephant weighs), is 13 feet long, and the barrel has a diameter of 20 inches at the end. (That's big enough for a child to crawl into!) It could fire a cannonball that weighed almost 400 pounds. It can be seen today at Edinburgh Castle in Scotland.

CHAPTER 7
More Than a Warrior

A knight didn't spend every minute of his life in battle. He spent way more time living at the castle, where much was expected of him. A knight was supposed to be able to play at least one instrument, and to sing, dance, and recite poetry. A knight might also learn how to read and write in his own language, as well as in Latin and perhaps even a foreign language. (Latin was the language used by the Christian church. All important books were written in Latin.) And of course he had to be generous, honorable, just, truthful, and use his strength to protect those weaker than him at all times.

The set of rules that a knight had to live by was called the code of chivalry. The word *chivalry* comes from an old French word *chevalerie*, which means "horse soldiering." But it came to mean more than just being a soldier on a horse. A knight had to set a good example. If he didn't and disgraced his lord, his sword and spurs were often taken away from him and broken.

A knight playing a lute

Knights were inspired to do deeds of chivalry to prove themselves worthy of the love of one of the ladies at court. This was known as courtly love.

Many of the ladies at court were already married, so courtly love was like a game. A knight might never win the lady's hand, but he kept battling for her love. Through courtly love, it was thought that a knight could perfect himself and reach the peak of knighthood.

Minstrels who traveled from castle to castle told stories about these "perfect" knights who were brave and honorable. As time went on, these stories were written down. The stories were tales of knights who had fought courageously and were examples of kindness and generosity. In France, the tales about knights were called *chansons de geste*, which means "songs of heroic deeds." Many of the stories were about real knights, such as

Richard the Lionheart

Richard the Lionheart of England. Some had started as true stories but became grander and more exaggerated each time they were retold, like the tales of King Arthur and the Knights of the Round Table. And some of the stories were made up, such as the tale of Perceval, who went on a quest to find the Holy Grail, the cup used by Jesus Christ at the Last Supper.

In these tales of valiant and loyal knights, the most romantic of all was a knight-errant. He was a knight who traveled around the country on his own looking for adventure. In reality, most knights stayed connected to the same lord their entire lives. Many of them got married and had children. Their sons may have become knights, and their daughters perhaps married knights.

La Chanson de Roland

La Chanson de Roland, which means *The Song of Roland*, was most likely written by a French poet named Turold around 1100. It was one of the earliest *chansons de geste* to be written down, and is considered to be one of the greatest.

The song is over four thousand lines long and tells the story of Roland, a knight in the army of a king named Charlemagne. In the song, Roland's stepfather, Ganelon, comes up with a plan to have his stepson, whom he dislikes, killed as the army travels home to France after fighting in Spain. Ganelon tells the enemy army that Roland will be traveling at the rear and that they should ambush him and the other soldiers.

As Roland and his fellow knights come under attack, one of his friends tells him to blow his horn. The horn will signal that they need help. But Roland does not want to be seen as a coward and he says they can fight off the enemy. Roland and his friends fight bravely, but in the end they are defeated. Before he dies, Roland does blow his horn so that Charlemagne can see what happened and take revenge on the enemy.

Roland chose death over shame. *La Chanson de Roland* became extremely popular and is still performed today. In fact, it is considered the national poem of France.

CHAPTER 8
Tournaments

When they weren't fighting, knights still had to keep up their skills. They needed to be prepared to go to battle at a moment's notice. Also, many knights liked fighting. They were trained for battle and often had a violent streak. So to help knights stay fit and blow off steam, a lord would hold an event called a tournament.

These organized events often lasted for days. At a tournament, knights fought each other in mock battles, either one against one or as part of a team. When a lord announced that a tournament would take place, hundreds of squires and knights might take part. People from far and wide would come to watch the knights fight. Going to a tournament was like going to a sporting event or a music festival. Knights were who successful at tournaments were the sports stars or rock stars of their day.

At a tournament, tents would be set up and there would be people selling farm animals, food, armor, weapons, and lots of other things. Storytellers, minstrels, acrobats, and musicians would come and entertain the crowds. Stands were built where the ladies of the court would sit. Dressed in their best gowns, they cheered on their favorite knights.

Tournaments in the eleventh and twelfth centuries had melees (say: MAY-lays). These mock battles took place over a large area of land, and there were two teams fighting to win. A melee was usually not supervised and often became

violent. Knights were sometimes killed during a melee. By the thirteenth century, melees became more organized. Strict rules were put in place, and knights used blunt weapons.

By the fourteenth century, melees were replaced by jousts. They were much safer and easier to organize and supervise. Plus, it was easier to see a knight's skill when he was fighting one-on-one, instead of in a large group racing around on horseback. In a joust, two knights in armor faced each other in head-to-head combat. Each was armed with a long lance, and they charged at each other down a long track called

a list. Each wanted to throw his opponent off his horse. The winner of each joust would move on to compete with other winners until there was only one undefeated knight. From about 1400, jousting knights rode on either side of a barrier called a tilt. The tilt prevented the horses

from running into each other. Special armor was developed for tournament jousts. It was reinforced in the areas where a knight might be hit by his opponent. It was also heavier and less flexible than battle armor, which made it hard to move. However, knights didn't have it on for very long.

In a joust, the faces of knights were covered by heavy helmets. (A jousting helmet was often three times heavier than a battle helmet.) Very often, a jousting helmet was decorated with plumes (feathers) or horns. Even though their faces weren't visible, spectators knew each knight by his armor, helmet, or shield with his coat of arms.

The judges of the jousts as well as the lords and ladies looked on from the stands where they had a good view. Poorer spectators stood below the stands. The stands were decorated with banners and tapestries. The spectators in the stands often threw coins to show which knight they wanted to win.

Another reason knights enjoyed tournaments was that they could make money. The winner of a joust might win a prize, such as a jewel, a gold chain, a sword, or a hawk trained for hunting. And a defeated knight sometimes had to give up his armor and horse to the winner.

A knight wins money after a tournament.

As time went on, tournaments became less about practicing battle skills and more about having a good time. Knights would often dress in costumes for their jousts. They would fight dressed as ancient Romans, monks, or even women. Sometimes they dressed up as knights from legends. Jousts were even held on the water. Dueling knights would do battle with each other from boats.

Jousting Kings

Knights weren't the only men who took part in tournaments. By the fourteenth century, many noblemen, including kings, tested their skill, talent, and bravery in jousts. And they were often injured, just like their knights.

King Henry VIII of England took part in many tournaments. But in 1536, he severely injured his

King Henry VIII

leg during a joust. Henry, who was in full armor, was thrown from his horse. His horse, which was also in full armor, fell on top of him. His leg was badly wounded. It is said that after the accident, Henry went from being generous and kind to being cruel and suspicious.

In 1559, King Henry II of France took part in a joust to celebrate his daughter's marriage. During the joust, a sliver from his opponent's lance broke off, pierced one of his eyes, and killed him. Royalty stopped participating in jousts, and eventually France outlawed jousting.

CHAPTER 9
Knighthood's End

At the height of the Middle Ages, the feudal system ordered the way most people in Europe lived. But that all changed by the end of the fifteenth century. There were new types of weapons that could destroy a castle and kill knights no matter what kind of armor they wore. Rather than pay for knights living at their castle, even in times of peace, kings and lords began to depend on paid soldiers. There were fewer noblemen to carry on the code of chivalry. Because of this, fewer people followed the feudal system and its traditions.

Gunpowder was first used in a major Western European battle at the Battle of Crécy in 1346. After that, it was used more and more often in battles and in war. Castles could not withstand the power of bigger and better cannons that used gunpowder. Also, a suit of armor could not protect a knight from the harquebus (say: HAR-kwuh-bus), a gun fired from the shoulder that was similar to a rifle. Guns, not

A man firing a harquebus

knights, came to rule the battlefield.

Over time, lords began paying trained foot soldiers to fight in battles. Men fought for a fee. They didn't fight for just one lord, either. In fact, after fighting for one lord, they might later fight for his enemy. Plus, going to battle with an army of knights on horseback became too costly. It was less expensive and easier for a lord to hire an army of skilled men armed with pikes, lances, and halberds. They could hold off a charge of horses from an enemy.

Toward the end of the Middle Ages, there were fewer young boys who took the path of page to squire to knight. Fewer families could afford this career for their sons. Also, some young men did not want to have to fight for a living when they could do other, less dangerous things.

Since castles no longer provided certain protection from new weapons, in time the lords moved out of them. Castles were no longer the center of activity in an area. Instead, many people chose to live in villages, towns, and cities. These places became the seat of government. People no longer needed the protection of a lord and his castle.

By the 1600s, the great age of castles and knights was at an end. But its ideals of chivalry, its legends, and its heroes live on to this day.

Take a Tour

   Although for centuries many castles were left in ruins, many others around the world still stand and can be visited today.

   Eilean Donan—one of the most famous castles in Scotland, it stands on an island where three sea lakes meet.

Eilean Donan

Himeji Castle—this castle stands on a hill overlooking Himeji, Japan. Building started in the early 1300s, and it was under construction off and on for nearly three hundred years.

Alcázar of Segovia—this beautiful castle in Spain has served as a royal palace, a prison, and a military school.

Eltz Castle—this castle in Germany is still owned by a branch of the family that lived there in the twelfth century.

Windsor Castle—this castle in England is a home of Queen Elizabeth II and is the biggest castle still used as a residence.

Timeline of Castles and Knights

800	Charlemagne, king of the Franks, is crowned emperor of the Holy Roman Empire
c. 850	First motte-and-bailey castles built
1000s	New class of soldiers with armor and horses, known as knights, develops in parts of Western Europe
1066	Normans from northern France invade England and introduce a feudal system
1100s	Knights begin adding more mail to their armor to protect their arms and legs; a code of conduct, known as chivalry, is adopted by all knights; first tournaments, knows as melees, are held
1300s	Knights add steel plates to their armor; cannons appear on battlefields and during sieges
1337–1453	The Hundred Years' War between England and France, which includes the battles of Crécy (1346) and Agincourt (1415)
1400s	Knights begin to wear full suits of plate armor for full-body protection
1431	Joan of Arc is put to death
1500s	Paid soldiers and armies begin to replace armies of knights
1559	French king Henry II killed in a joust

Timeline of the World

476 —	Fall of the Western Roman Empire in Europe
c. 570 —	Birth of the prophet Muhammad
c. 700 —	The Maya civilization in Central America reaches its peak
c. 860 —	Vikings discover Iceland
1000 —	Viking explorer Leif Erikson sails from Greenland to North America
1117 —	The University of Oxford is founded
c. 1200 —	Cambodia's Khmer Empire reaches its height
1206 —	Genghis Khan becomes ruler of Mongolia
1215 —	Magna Carta is signed in England
1235 —	The Empire of Mali in West Africa is established
1271 —	Marco Polo travels from Italy to China, returns in 1295
1347–1453 —	The plague, or "Black Death," sweeps across Europe
1400s —	The Aztecs build their empire in Mexico
c. 1450 —	Johannes Gutenberg completes a moveable-type printing press in Europe
1492 —	Christopher Columbus sails from Spain to the New World

Bibliography

*Books for young readers

Carr, Helen. "10 Facts About Medieval Castles," *History Hit*, July 30, 2018. https://www.historyhit.com/facts-about-medieval-castles/.

*Coggins, Jack. *The Illustrated Book of Knights*. Mineola, NY: Dover Publications, 2006.

*Evans, Tom. *A Look at . . . the Age of Knights and Castles*. Chicago: World Book, 2011.

Gies, Frances. *The Knight in History*. New York: Harper & Row, 1984.

Gies, Joseph and Frances. *Life in a Medieval Castle*. New York: Harper & Row, 1974.

*Gravett, Christopher. *Eyewitness: Knight*. New York: DK Publishing, 1993.

*Hinds, Kathryn. *Life in the Middle Ages: The Castle*. Tarrytown, NY: Benchmark Books, 2001.

Jestice, Phyllis. *The Medieval Knight*. London: Amber Books, 2018.

*Matthews, Rupert. *Knights and Castles*. New York: DK Publishing, 2016.

*Maynard, Christopher. *Days of the Knights: A Tale of Castles and Battles*. New York: DK Publishing, 1998.

Phillips, Charles. *Knights & the Golden Age of Chivalry*. London: Southwater, 2017.

*Templeman, Henry. *Knights: Secrets of Medieval Warriors*. London: Carlton Books, 2015.

Websites

ancient.eu/Medieval_Knight

ducksters.com/history/middle_ages/history_of_knights.php

exploring-castles.com/castle_life/

medievalchronicles.com/medieval-knights/medieval-knights-history/

pbswesternreserve.org/education/middle-ages/